Pamela Anderson

In Pictures

Pamela Anderson

In Pictures

photographs
by

Stephen
Wayda

Text by Bibi Jordan

General Publishing Group

GPG

Los Angeles

Publisher, W. Quay Hays
Managing Editor, Colby Allerton
Art Director, Kurt Wahlner
Projects Manager, Trudihope Schlomowitz
Production Director, Nadeen Torio
Color & Pre-Press Director, Gaston Moraga
Production Artist, Phillis Stacy
Production Assistants, Tom Archibeque, Alan Peak
Copy Editor, Carolyn Wendt

Pamela Anderson In Pictures is published by:
General Publishing Group, Inc.
2701 Ocean Park Blvd., Ste. 140
Santa Monica, CA 90405

Copyright © 1996 by Chase Creek Productions, Inc.
Photographs © 1996 by Stephen Wayda

Library of Congress Cataloging-in-Publication Data

Wayda, Stephen.
   Pamela Anderson In Pictures / photographs by Stephen Wayda ; text by Bibi Jordan.
     p.   cm.
   ISBN 1-881649-94-6
   1. Anderson, Pamela--Portraits.   I. Jordan, Bibi.   II. Title
PN2308.A53W38 1996
791.45'028'092--dc20   96-3261
                              CIP

Credits:

Copy editors: Stephen Kingsley, Shane Boocock
Make-up & Hair: Alexis Vogel
Styling: Jennifer Tutor
Color processing: A&I Labs, Hollywood
Black & white prints: Phillip Nardulli, Hollywood
Cover coloring: Bill Castillo, Gaston Moraga and Phillis A. Stacy

Dedicated to:

To Karen and Madison, whose beauty outshines the stars: SW
To Alexandra and John, my incentive and inspiration: BJ

Acknowledgments:

A woman's beauty springs from her soul. In my photography, I try to capture a woman's inner light, illuminating her personal essence. Pamela's physical beauty is acknowledged by two billion fans worldwide—but working with her over the years, it was her personality, drive and energy that I found unique, inspiring me to share this tribute to Pamela with her fans around the world.

I wish to thank four key individuals who spearheaded my career: Henry H. Carter, my grandfather, who gave me a dream; Brent Herridge, photographer and friend, who gave me my initial start; Dwight Hooker, legendary *Playboy* photographer, who gave me my break and Ken Marcus, the best photographer I've ever known, who gave me my focus.

Of course, *Playboy* provided the ultimate lab to develop my art.
I am especially grateful to Hugh Hefner, who blessed me with the chance to photograph the world's most beautiful women, West Coast Photo Editor Marilyn Grabowski who relentlessly provided generous and perceptive criticism of my work, and Gary Cole who supplied constant encouragement and support.

I reserve special thanks to the "best of the best," my makeup artist Alexis Vogel and my stylist Jennifer Tutor, for their superb contribution in creating an image for the book—and for Pamela. I'm grateful to my crew for their devotion and companionship: assistants Kip Corby, David Goodman and Phil Shockley; stylists Lane Coyle Dunn and Fanny Freeman; and makeup artist Tracy Cicenflone. My appreciation of them as professionals and friends never ceases.

For sound counsel, I am indebted to Jim Roehig of Outline, Todd Moyer of Dark Horse Productions, David Livingstone of Polygram Film International, Dennis Brody of Ray Manzella Productions, Marcia Terrones and Tim Hawkins of *Playboy*, Ken Okazaski, Jonathan Kirsch, Bibi Jordan and Quay Hays.

And, last but not least, thanks to my family for waiting patiently for my return from assignments to replenish my soul with beauty,

Stephen Wayda

Foreword by Marilyn Grabowski
West Coast Photo Editor, *Playboy* Magazine

When she was growing up, Pam Anderson was the kind of girl that drew funny little "Have a Nice Day" faces next to her name, a girl who rounded and separated her letters very carefully. This would either indicate a very proper schooling or a girl who knew she was going to be a star and was practicing how she would write when she became famous.

Recently, I reread Pamela's Playmate Data Sheet dated January 29, 1989. Seven years ago, the 21-year-old green/gray-eyed blonde revealed her duality even then: She declared that she was a homebody who loved to cook, who was wild about being hugged and whose favorite music was Mozart. But she also admitted that she wanted to be an actress, loved to live out her fantasies, gravitated toward controversy, longed to portray different characters and wanted to make love to her fiancé in every country of the world.

When Canadian photographer Ken Honey first sent me Pamela's modeling composite from her hometown of Vancouver, I immediately brought her down for a cover shoot. Of course, I had an ulterior motive in mind; Pamela would be a brilliant choice for Playmate. It wasn't my practice to bring girls into town for cover shootings; we had so many beautiful girls living in L.A., it was a bit like bringing coals to Newcastle. But Pam's natural innocence, brilliant smile and inner spirit caught my eye immediately, and in person she was even lovelier than on film.

I remember saying to her over dinner at Spago that a celebrity future was there for her; she just had to make the effort. Heads turned and eyes followed her when she walked across the restaurant; she seemed oblivious to the attention. Paparazzi took her picture as we left the restaurant, even though they didn't know who she was.

Pamela wasn't at all comfortable doing nudes when we shot her Playmate centerfold. Yet she was good-humored and tried to cover up her embarrassment with the giggles she still manifests. I got to know her, and she became my friend.

Steve Wayda shot Pamela's Playmate test in May of 1989. I had first seen his work in the early eighties, when he sent me a not-particularly-successful shooting of a girl he had met in Utah, where he lived (and still does). However undeveloped his photography was, there was something about it that caught my eye, and I had him try another test shooting to see what he could do. He grew rapidly into one of the lucky chosen few to become a contributing photographer to *Playboy* magazine. After working with Steve for over 15 years, I have watched him become one of the top photographers of women in the world. He has the unique ability of combining sensuality with personality in a totally individual style.

Steve worked especially well with Pamela throughout the intervening years, photographing her for five covers—a record—between October 1989 through January 1996. *Playboy* obviously knew a good thing when they saw it, because Pamela boosted sales (and male blood pressure) whenever she appeared in the magazine. Soon Pam was using Steve for non-*Playboy* assignments, and the two of them made some kind of photography magic. He captured her beauty and personality as no other photographer ever had.

Men loved Pam. For a while, she lived with Scott Baio, and the home-cooking side of her nature took over. But that was not to be. Soon she was being sought after—downright chased—by some of the biggest names in town. But by then, with much prodding by me, she had decided to work on her career.

The rest is entertainment history. She had graduated from bit parts on "Married with Children" to becoming the irresistible "Tool Time" girl on "Home Improvement" when "Baywatch" beckoned. I'm not sure whether "Baywatch" did it for her, or whether she did it for "Baywatch." Both the show and Pamela soared in popularity, first internationally and then here in America.

Pamela was no doubt born under a brilliant shining star, singling her out from the pack. She creates publicity and notoriety wherever she goes, helped along by her whirlwind romance and marriage to tattooed rock star Tommy Lee. She cried in my office when, hospitalized for exhaustion, the tabloids had her overdosing on drugs. Several months later, she returned to the hospital, this time for a miscarriage. A short time ago, Pamela was once again hospitalized for exhaustion, finding out in the process that she was again pregnant.

And they lived happily ever after…or so we hope the story goes. How it will all play out, I cannot begin to predict. A legend, particularly in someone so young, isn't easy to sustain. But Pamela has beaten the odds before and, I suspect, she's still capable of a few surprises. Pamela Anderson can't help being a fascinating person. She's definitely worth watching.

"Beautiful and sexy,

she really knows how to make love with my camera. She's got that fire in her belly, which illuminates her face with personality and desire."

Top photographer Stephen Wayda recalls his glamour shoots with Pamela Anderson that have made her the most sensually happening siren on Earth.

More fame than Clinton, more raunch appeal

than Princess Di, the post-Barbie, sexually ballistic blonde ignites the fantasies of fans from California to Kathmandu with her just-swept-off-the-pillow hair, incendiary pout and come-cry-on-me cleavage. Pamela is a libido flow on legs, a testosterone trip in tights, pushing femininity to the max, deep within the male psyche.

Within reach, visually, of two billion global viewers through the sun-and-swimsuit stun-out, "Baywatch," Pamela has now stepped beyond the bounds of babedom and into another league. A TV temptress. A big-screen seductress. A glossy magazine goddess. Garbo, Bardot and Monroe? The nineties belong to Pamela.

Cosmically blessed at birth — July 1st, 1967: Canada's one-hundredth birthday — Pamela was less than 24 hours old when she first captured headlines — and hearts — as "British Columbia's Centennial Baby." Fairy tales came alive, again, when four years later she was sighted at a storytime hour by the Canadian Library System, which starred her in its national campaign. A dreamy adolescent bookworm, Pamela fantasized about being a romance novelist, never expecting she'd be the subject, not the author, of a runaway best-seller.

With a hop, a skip and a stiletto step, the man-magnet from Cosmox, British Columbia, has gone from high-school hopeful to *über* babe within a matter of years.

Indeed, Pamela's first media appearance came six years ago on the big screen at a Canadian football game where a cameraman zoomed in on her bulging blouse with its Labatt's logo and shared the dramatic sight with the crowd. Flashed around the stadium, the image induced fever-pitch passion and led to a nationwide Labatt's poster campaign, literally fronted by the new pinup.

A Playboy scout then spotted her slinking around

near one of the ad hoardings and immediately proposed that she pose for his magazine's college issue. Soon, instead of bearing the northern Canadian cold, Pamela was baring all south of the border.

"That girl was magic!" *Playboy*'s West Coast vice president and photo editor Marilyn Grabowoski remembers in the magazine's best-selling video on Pamela Anderson. "I initially wanted her as a Playmate but offered her a cover and said, 'You can be very successful. You can be a star, a celebrity, whatever you want...You've got it!'"

PLAYBOY

ENTERTAINMENT FOR MEN

OCTOBER 1989 • $4.00

GIRLS OF THE SOUTHEASTERN CONFERENCE

KEITH RICHARDS INTERVIEW

JULIE McCULLOUGH PICTORIAL YOU WON'T SEE HER LIKE THIS ON *GROWING PAINS*

PLAYBOY'S FEARLESS PIGSKIN PREVIEW

COLLEGE WOMEN TALK STRAIGHT ABOUT CAMPUS SEX

BOLD BACK TO CAMPUS ISSUE

At the initial Playboy shoot,

Pamela's principal photographer, Stephen Wayda, was knocked out by his first glimpse of the future "Baywatch" beauty, clad in traditional Ivy League-style blazer, college tie and knee socks.

"She was the quintessential college girl, with long straight sandy hair and a cute figure, every college boy's dream," he recalls. "She had the innocence of an ingenue combined with a natural easy sensuality."

It was during that original *Playboy* cover shoot that Wayda realized Pamela was different. At Grabowski's suggestion, arrangements were made to bare all in a centerfold test shooting, and not only did she take to de-clothing like a duck to water but proceeded to paddle a bit too eagerly for the mainstream mag.

"We had to keep telling Pamela to be less revealing," explains Wayda. "*Playboy* has its own style, which is more about sensuality than sex, and we have special ways to position women for the centerfold. But she was very sexy and, in any pose, was really hot."

Centerfold shoots

are usually a pain in the shapely ass for models. Shot with an 8 x 10 camera with a one-inch critical focus range, and involving over 30 separate lighting units, they usually last a passion-sapping week.

Every inch of the set is carefully conceived for maximum fantasy intensity, from the ruffle on the teddy to the folds in the sexy satin sheets, while the model's bunny-soft glow and eye-massaging curves are accentuated by highlights and smoky shadows. During the intricate preparation of the first few days, femmes fatales are often reduced to near dummy status in the studio, and at the call for "action," they can come on like wet blankets rather than carnal fireworks. Pamela was raw, but raring.

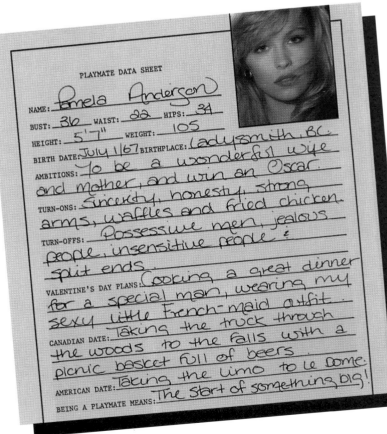

PLAYMATE DATA SHEET

NAME: Pamela Anderson
BUST: 36 WAIST: 22 HIPS: 34
HEIGHT: 5'7" WEIGHT: 105
BIRTH DATE: July 1/67 BIRTHPLACE: Ladysmith, BC.
AMBITIONS: To be a wonderful wife and mother, and win an Oscar.
TURN-ONS: Sincerity, honesty, strong arms, waffles and fried chicken.
TURN-OFFS: Possessive men, jealous people, insensitive people & split ends.
VALENTINE'S DAY PLANS: Cooking a great dinner for a special man, wearing my sexy little French-maid outfit.
CANADIAN DATE: Taking the truck through the woods to the falls with a picnic basket full of beers.
AMERICAN DATE: Taking the limo to Le Dome.
BEING A PLAYMATE MEANS: The start of something big!

"When I was ready to shoot, she really turned on her concentration and allure," says Wayda. "She was very aware of her body, its strengths and weaknesses. Probably, Pamela considers her hair as her greatest asset and uses it like a prop. And she knows the power of her eyes — she can talk with her eyes!"

But her tongue tells of faults, too.

"Pamela always feels she's too heavy, but I'm always encouraging her to add a little more roundness to her body," laughs Wayda. "And she also thinks that she's short in the legs, so I have special ways to dress and shoot her to give those legs an extra long look."

But when the new cover queen saw the results of that first steamy session, her concerns vanished.

"When I saw the *Playboy* pictures,

I was totally shocked. I had no idea how beautiful they were going to look," she told fans in a later *Playboy* video, while confessing in a *Sky* magazine interview, "I was really nervous because people are told that it's wrong and that you have to wear some clothes, but after a while it became really fun. I mean, I've always been kind of modest, but it was good because it really built my self-confidence. I enjoyed doing the pictures and I've enjoyed seeing them in print."

For Wayda, it was in the freer environment of the small-camera shoot that Pamela came into her erotic own, rather than in the tripod-taken teases.

"When I photograph a woman, I want to capture her sense of self, the power of her sexuality, the imagination of her fantasies, and the model has to give one hundred percent of her personality, concentration and drive," he explains. "I can create magic with light, makeup and wardrobe and I can complement and magnify feeling. But only the model can turn up the light that makes the difference — the light behind her eyes."

For Pamela

"sexuality is an expression of spirituality" and she credits her grandfather, a Finnish emigrant, for opening her mind. Now she meditates and, ever since he explained that her dreams would uncover her destiny, all the capers of her unconscious are recorded dutifully. And there must be some pretty wild chapters coming to life!

Indeed, Stephen Wayda has seen Pamela's dreams unfold in real time from a fresh young schoolgirl to the sex icon of the nineties and believes that her rise to fame is no accident.

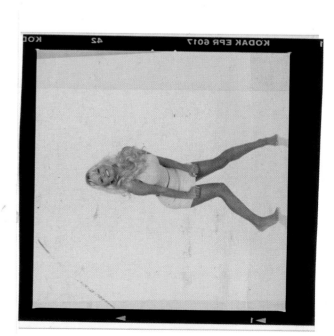

"What really sets Pamela apart from all the other beautiful models I've photographed is that she has a very clear vision of where she wants to go and who she wants to be," he argues. "She wanted to break out of the confines of the backwaters of Vancouver and get everything she could out of life.

"She was driven from the start and has always taken herself and her career very seriously and worked like a professional," he adds. "That's why she always hits the roof whenever anyone calls her 'babe.'"

So don't call Pamela "babe."

Like Pamela, Wayda also attributes ambition, serendipity and the guidance of his grandfather — a Beverly Hills interior decorator and a fanatic photographer during the Golden Age of Hollywood — to his success. Originally a reporter on a small Utah newspaper, Wayda's focus changed with a gift from his grandfather.

"He left me his Leica camera, which opened my eyes to a new life," he explains. "And with it I found that my grandfather had also bequeathed his photographer's eye and joie de vivre. Photographing models was a great way

for a shy guy to meet lots of beautiful women!"

After studying his creative camera craft at the University of Utah, Wayda started collaborating with an aspiring talent scout, Susie McCarty, whose agency grew to be the biggest in Utah, and commercial photographer Brett Henridge, who was then handling advertising assignments for the city's top department store.

"We had a great time. Together we were fashion in Salt Lake City," the hip photographer remembers. "We were the big fish in a little pond, but we worked hard, doing all our own processing and printing, often until four A.M."

Having established himself,

Wayda met *Playboy*'s retiring Dwight Hooker, who at first didn't reckon the new camera kid had what it took to turn on the male nation. But with persistent pleading, Wayda persuaded Hooker to accept an apprentice, assign test shoots and critique the results.

"After a couple of years of photographing any models who would pose for me as *Playboy* test shots, I finally found two Utah women that *Playboy* wanted as centerfolds," Wayda reminisces. "Marilyn gave me my big break — the deal was one woman was to be shot by Ken Marcus and I'd be able to watch. The second girl was to be my shooting.

"I was really lucky to observe Ken. He's the most technically brilliant photographer I've ever encountered — he taught me everything about photographing centerfolds," Wayda explains. "Thanks to his instruction, on my first try, I succeeded doing what no one else had done in fifteen years, or has been able to do in the last eighteen years — master the technique of centerfold photography."

Wayda, with his eye for female allure, was soon hired and is now one of only three principal photographers working on the world-famous mag. To date, he's created over 76 *Playboy* covers, some 35 centerfolds and an orgy of pictorials.

He commutes to *Playboy*'s Santa Monica studio from his horse ranch in Park City, Utah, where he lives with his wife, Karen, and three children, Chase, Morgan, and Madison. And when he's not horning up the world's most wanted women in exotic locations, he's racing down a polo field with his team, Chase Creek, named after his production company.

Just as

Wayda's first centerfold launched his career, Pamela's first public exposure also developed new career directions. She broke into TV with a bit part as the "Tool Time" girl on "Home Improvement" and from there dived straight into "Baywatch" as C.J., the lusty lifeguard in the curve-caressing, fire-engine-red swimsuit.

Twenty percent of the world's population were tuned in

and turned on as Pamela bounced across the sand leaving dudes looking like doped-out dogs in her heated wake. "Baywatch" was post-feminist fantasy a-go-go: A stunning golden-haired maiden rescues strong men, powerless in her arms and under her charms. The metaphor screams from the scenes.

"A super-sexy amalgam of hormones and Coppertone," wrote *People* while Britain's *Daily Mirror* enthused that no male was immune: "Among the avid viewers are academics with sky-high IQs...After an hour in front of 'Baywatch,' back they go, suitably inspired by Pamela Anderson's cleavage, to work on splitting the atom or to write the great British novel."

At first, Pamela loved the dumb-blonde image.

"I have nothing to live up to," she told *People.* "I can only surprise people."

34

Eventually tiring of the one-dimensional beach-bunny wiggle-fest, Pamela asked for help nailing down a new persona, and her makeup artist, Alexis Vogel, had the idea to transform her into a nineties Brigitte Bardot, who was at the time tied with Bo Derek as *Playboy* magazine's most prolific cover girl.

The French former sex-kitten's birthplace, St. Tropez, was chosen for the shoot that would shatter Derek and Bardot's record and launch Pamela on a passion offensive with an even more provocative image.

▶7A 8 ▶8A
DAK 5053 TMY 14 KODAK 5053 TMY 15

▶13A 14 ▶14A 15
5053 TMY 20 KODAK 5053 TMY 2

▶19A 19 ▶19A 20 ▶20A 2
KODAK 5053 TMY 25 KODAK 5053 TMY 26 KODAK 5053 TMY 27

▶24A 25 ▶25A 26 ▶26A 27
ODAK 5053 TMY 31 KODAK 5053 TMY 32 KODAK 5053 TMY 33

KODAK

9A   10
DAK 5053 TMY   16

KODAK

15A   16
DAK 5053 TMY   22

21A   22   22A   23   23A   24
DAK 5053 TMY   28   KODAK 5053 TMY   29   KODAK 5053 TMY   30

27A   28   28A   29   29A   30
DAK 5053 TMY   34   KODAK 5053 TMY   35   KODAK 5053 TMY   36

Alexis sculpted new erotic
signposts onto Pamela's features. Long flirtatious lashes,
a soft sultry pout and a big
flouncy blond mane turned up
the volume of her allure. Now,
instead of softly whispering
"sex," she was
screaming it. And, on the
Mediterranean shore

"La Sirene de Malibu"

was recognized everywhere.

"Wherever we went, everyone knew Pam,"

remembers Fanny Freeman, *Playboy*'s wardrobe coordinator. "One day we were shooting at a bistro when a busload of kids stopped to watch us work. One bold boy went up to Pamela for an autograph and suddenly there was a feeding frenzy of them, all chanting, 'Pamela! Pamela! Pamela!'"

For the photo session,

Fanny selected erotically incendiary outfits that made the most of Pamela's assets. Cinched up in a French bustier in one shot, laced up in six-inch sandals in another, the new nymph on the block became a delicatessen of yin essence. Gazing lazily from a fancy balcony window, Pamela tempts. Wearing a crotch-high, thigh-tight white mini, she dares. And naked, bar a floppy hat and a smile, she teases.

At night, too, Pamela lived up to the Bardot legend, beating the early curfew Wayda had set to go out on the town with Alexis, checking out the French Riviera beach boys.

In spite of 4:00 A.M. wake up calls, the *Playboy* photographer never realized

Pamela was staying up late.

"Regardless of the start time, she was always one hundred percent on," he explains. "Because the harbor of St. Tropez faces east, sunrise was the optimum time to shoot as the early morning sea mist gave the light a soft diffuse look that cast a golden glow to Pamela's skin."

While the French resort dwellers

slept off hangovers, Pamela skipped on red-tiled rooftops and balanced on brightly painted fishing boats in harbor coves. Then, while scouting in exclusive beach clubs for new locations, she fell for the cutest beach boy in town and was soon asking Wayda to use him in the shoot so she could spend more time in his arms.

Wayda planned a sunrise shot of the two, swathed in creamy satin sheets and bathed in dawn's pink rays filtered through gently wafting curtains. Pamela's beau finally showed up, still warm and tousled from oversleep, and the pair got to work.

"Pamela was positively pining for her man," recalls Wayda. "She'd been dating him for several days and was getting really frustrated with the chaperone and the schedule. I'd only agreed to Pamela's request for him to be in the shoot on condition that they wait another day to spend time alone together. So there was a tremendous sexual tension,

especially when they were both naked.

"But Pamela was a real pro," he adds. "She was perfectly in control and very conscious of the position her body was in and how to move his without getting out of hand. *Playboy* editors told me they had never seen such passion in a couple shoot."

The only thing hotter

than the sands of St. Tropez that summer was Pamela's pictorial hot off the press. The beach babe became a sex bombshell and glossy mags the world over clamored for more photos. Pamela Anderson, former Canadian football fan, was now the most lusted-after female in the world.

KODAK 5053 TMY

When the top European youth magazine, *Sky*, commissioned Wayda to produce a major fashion/lifestyle spread, Pamela's body was styled to even loftier heights.

Galaxy glam goddess

Pamela dangled

a diamond necklace provocatively above her slightly puckered mouth as she lay draped in a gossamer satin gown, or teased herself with a pink feather boa. And out on the L.A. town, Pamela posed publicly in six-inch shrieking red stilettos and black vinyl pants as she sucked popsicles and licked cotton candy for the camera.

When Sky appeared

featuring the photos, it was instantly snapped up from newsstands and became the best selling issue ever. The editor declared that even with all the celebrities *Sky* features, they had never had such success in terms of revenue or demand.

The demand for a piece of Pamela went on. And on.

And on. "Girls laugh at Pamela 'cause she's not Meryl Streep but boy are they missing the point," wrote journalist Stephen Kingston in a *Sky* editorial. "We need her. We need a pouting, teasing pinup to worship when we bond with our mates to reassert our waning masculinity. We need the security of a sex-bomb icon when we're watching our macho identity go down the plug hole while doing the washing up, while we look on with amazement as women get the top qualifications and jobs...as our safe world gets swept away by the radical tide of change. We need Pamela Anderson like we've never needed her before."

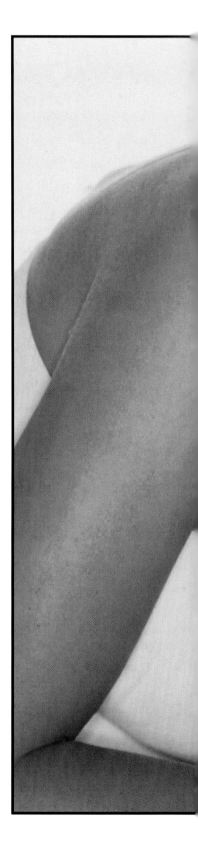

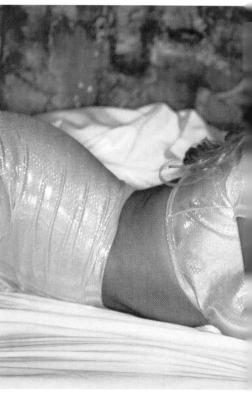

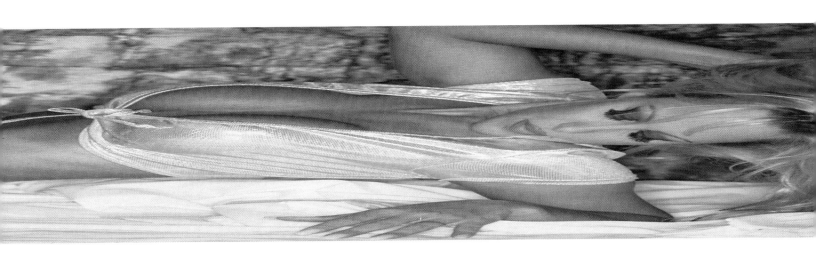

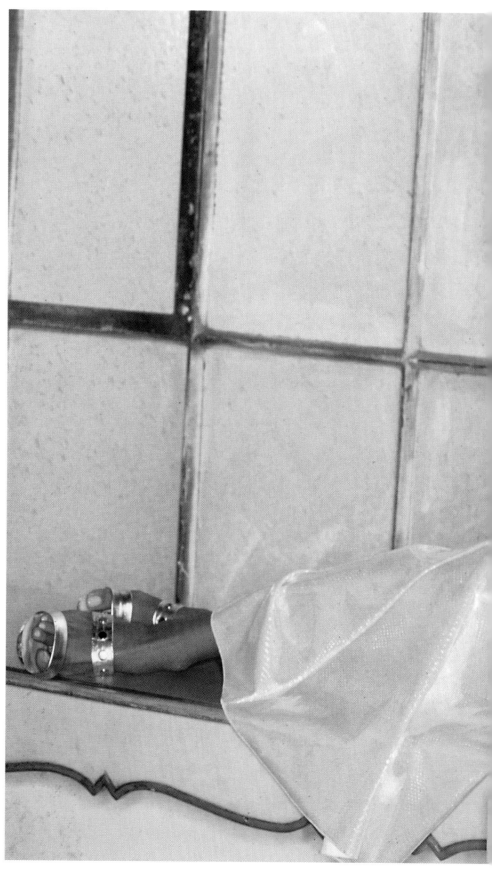

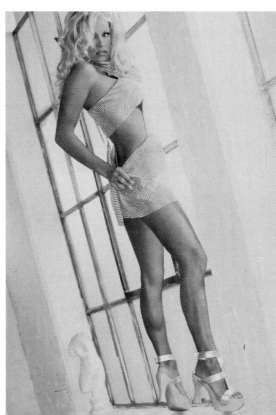

Together with Wayda,

she did another series of glamour shots that were printed around the world. But her fans' favorite erotic scenario was of the oiled, sun-kissed, scantily clad, swim-suited lifesaver cavorting on the beach, only too happily reprovided by a company who hired Pamela to promote their tanning lotion. Cancun, on the Mexican Gulf, was chosen as the location for the shoot.

"Our first day was awful," Wayda shudders. "The beach was packed and the high-rises blocked the sunset."

Instead, the crew shunned the tourist traps, retreating to a site where surf-pounded boulders deterred onlookers. Tuning into the elements, as Pamela slipped a dress over her sun-oiled, shimmering nudity,

Wayda was awestruck

for an enchanted moment.

"She was suddenly transformed into a mermaid," he

sighs. "She was like a sea goddess rising out of the rocks, a golden light illuminating her face, the surf spraying on her arched back and the wind whipping her wet body."

The Vision

set the tone for the remainder of the shoot, Wayda posing Pamela stretched out on the shore line, the waves crashing behind her and sea foam rolling up her body.

"In one set-up

we had Pamela dressed in a skin-tight long black latex gown, which looked great clinging to her body, the darkness contrasting with her creamy skin and wet blond hair," Wayda enthuses. "I wanted to bring out the animal in her so I told her to get down and snake through the wet sand. She was coming on like a sea creature emerging from the ocean, when a rock snagged the latex, which suddenly peeled back and disintegrated to reveal her bare body like some mythological being morphing from her cocoon."

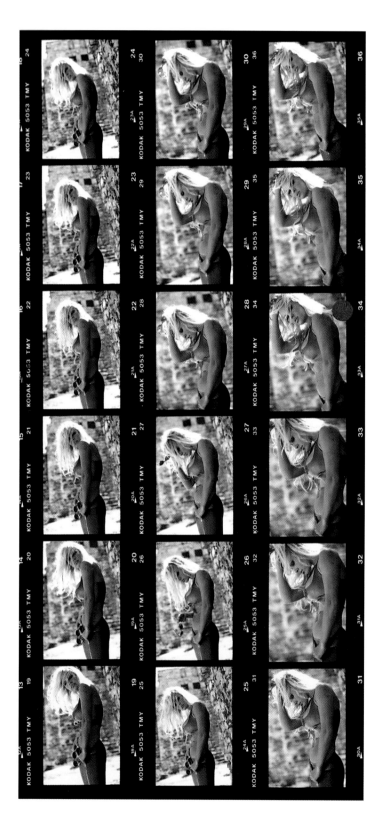

Sunning on the beach or scampering over ancient Mayan ruins, Pamela was steaming up more than Wayda's lenses. Returning to her hotel, she received word that an American, so impressed by a momentary meeting in L.A., had followed her to Cancun and was desperate for a romantic rendezvous. The guy was so pushy that Wayda asked Pamela if she wanted the interloper arrested. But finally the visitor's persistence paid off and Pamela agreed to meet him and his friend for a quick drink.

Arriving at the bar, she walked up to the wild-looking wanderlust victim and asked, "Are you Tommy Lee?" Less than 12 hours later she was engaged to the 32-year-old Motley Crue drummer.

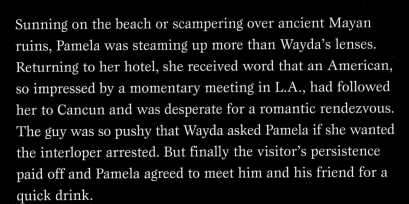

Pamela had first met Tommy

on the previous New Year's Eve and she told *TV Guide* that he had spent the evening licking her face. The heavy metal musician was insistent on getting her phone number, which was resisted at first but then handed over when Pamela realized that she was indeed attracted to him. Even so, when he called to ask for a date, she stood him up.

Then, as Pamela was leaving her house to catch the plane to Cancun, Tommy rang and she told him not to follow her to the Mexican shoot.

Too late. Once in Cancun, she was inundated with messages...

"It's Tommy Lee. Give me five minutes' notice and I'll come down and see you."

And then: "I'm on my way."

And then: "I'm here. I'm gonna look for you."

On Pamela's last day at the resort she called him.

"I figured, 'What could go wrong?'"
she told the *TV Guide* reporter. "We'd just go out to dinner and have a lot of fun."

"But that night we were inseparable...

And for the next few days. Obviously, we decided to stay. No one could pry us apart."

Everything promised by Pamela's eyes in those glossy, steamy photo shoots was poured into Tommy's existence as he got to live out a billion boys' bedroom fantasies.

"Making love to Tommy

seemed like the most natural and perfect thing to do. I knew I was madly in love with him," Pamela later told the London *Sun*. "That first time was incredible. Tommy satisfied me in a way no man has ever done before. We made love morning, noon and night…and sometimes morning, mid-morning, noon, afternoon, evening and midnight."

136

Like a nineties fairy tale,

the trip climaxed with a whirlwind wedding on the Cancun beach as the pair became a celebrity legal item and the media homed in. All Pamela could do was grin and bare it…with her photographer beside the nuptial bed.

"Pamela was dying for some intimate photos with Tommy, so she arranged for him to join us," Wayda explains. "When he came in, she seductively put her arms around him, slid her hands under his T-shirt and lovingly peeled it off. Tommy whispered to her, unsure of what was going on…and what was coming off!"

"She was bewildering

— and bewitching — him," Wayda adds. "Looking Tommy steadily in the eye, she slowly stripped down naked, wrapped her body around his and pulled him down onto the bed. Always such a natural in front of the camera, Pamela positioned her body perfectly for the camera, kissing and fondling him, using her body to ease him into the best positions."

"You could see

that they were totally enamored with each other and even forgot I was there. But I just did my thing and shot my fill, recording them crazy in love with each other until even I found it too hot to go on."

The wedding session

was followed by an impromptu celebration with champagne and a four-tiered cake with the crew. This time the event ended with cream smeared over everyone's faces as Pamela and company went loco.

"We're perfectly compatible," Pamela crooned to *TV Guide*. "We both have a crazy, wild side and also a compassionate, romantic side. Neither one of us thought that we'd ever get married, yet I meet this person and we get engaged the first night we're together. Four days later we're married. And it's the best thing I've ever done in my whole life!"

They keep their romance burning

with candlelight, champagne and rose-petal-strewn baths and bedsheets. And Tommy confesses that he gets hot every time he sees Pamela's silver-ringed second toe, while she gets turned on by his tattoos, so much so that she suggested they both get their wedding fingers branded. Meanwhile, as the press splashed the nuptial news of the beach babe and the beat boy, the ink was already drying on another contract — for Pamela to play the fetish female lead in the $15 million sci-fi fantasy, *Barb Wire*.

As her fame swelled,

so did her entourage. Accompanying Pamela this time on photo shoots for the film was a cast of over 30.

"The catering, a required line item dictated by the producer, cost even more than the studio rental," Wayda recalls.

After completing all the scripted shots, involving a missile-firing motorcycle and an attack-trained Rottweiler, the crowd dispersed, leaving Pamela alone with the photographer and crew.

"We started to improvise,"

explains Wayda. "I got Pamela down on the ground and she started rolling around with the gun. That's when we got the shot that was chosen for the film poster and the billboard."

In *Barb Wire*, Pamela is the ultimate icon for the nineties. A Barbarella/Bardot meltdown who sprays attitude and bullets like confetti. A post-emotional, post-prudent, gun-toting, tit-thrusting, hard-riding femme double fatale.

From baby doll to pinup,

beach babe to big-screen bombshell, Pamela has lived all the dreams that her grandfather predicted would come true. The shy schoolgirl who peeked provocatively into Wayda's lens just a few years ago is now a radical leather-clad sexual conquistador who glares invincibly from the silver screen, her own character merging with her screen persona as she admonishes the entire world…